THE WORLD OF Y
IN-DEPTH LOOK AT TURKISH OIL
WRESTLING

Understanding Its Cultural Roots, Unique Maneuvers, and Practical Defense Methods for Contemporary Wrestlers

By

Author:

Whalen Kwon-Ling

Contributor:

Thomas H. Fletcher

The World of Yagli Gures: An In-Depth Look at Turkish Oil Wrestling

Yağlı Güreş, or Turkish oil wrestling, is a traditional sport deeply rooted in Turkish culture. This book explores its cultural significance and unique traditions. Originating in ancient times, Yağlı Güreş has evolved while maintaining its core values and customs. The sport symbolizes honor, strength, and community, celebrated through various tournaments and festivals during the wrestling season.

Yağlı Güreş, or Turkish oil wrestling, is a traditional sport deeply rooted in Turkish culture. This book explores its origins, cultural significance, and unique traditions. Originating in ancient times, Yağlı Güreş has evolved while maintaining its core values and customs. The sport symbolizes honor, strength, and community, celebrated through various tournaments and festivals during the wrestling season.

Key rituals and iconic tournaments, such as the Kirkpinar Oil Wrestling Festival, highlight the sport's global appeal. Notable wrestlers inspire new generations, with rigorous training emphasizing physical and mental strength. The distinctive leather pants, known as "kıspet," are symbolic of the sport's tradition.

Music and drumming play a crucial role, adding excitement to matches. Modern adaptations have helped the sport evolve while retaining its essence, gaining international recognition. This book offers an insightful look into Yağlı Güreş, ensuring its future as a cherished cultural heritage.

Table of Content

Introduction

Yağlı güreş, known as oil wrestling, is a traditional Turkish sport. It dates back to ancient times, possibly as far back as the early days of the Ottoman Empire. This sport involves wrestlers, called pehlivan, who cover their bodies with olive oil. The oil makes it challenging to grip and control the opponent. This unique aspect adds a layer of difficulty and excitement to the sport.

The wrestling matches usually take place outdoors on grassy fields. These events are often part of larger festivals and celebrations. The most famous of these festivals is the annual Kırkpınar tournament held in Edirne, Turkey. This tournament is one of the oldest sports competitions in the world, with a history stretching back over 650 years.

In a typical match, wrestlers wear leather trousers called kıspet. These trousers are handmade and designed to withstand the rigors of the sport. The matches begin with the wrestlers dousing themselves in olive oil. This tradition is not only practical but also symbolic, representing purity and the sacredness of the competition.

The rules of yağlı güreş are simple yet demanding. A match can be won by pinning the opponent's back to the ground, lifting and carrying them for a certain distance, or getting them into a position where they can no longer fight back. The matches have no time limit, which can make them lengthy and physically exhausting.

Training to become a pehlivan requires dedication and discipline. Wrestlers often start training at a young age. The training regimen includes not only physical conditioning but also learning techniques and strategies specific to oil wrestling. Strength, agility, and endurance are crucial for success in this sport.

Respect and sportsmanship are fundamental values in yağlı güreş. Wrestlers show respect to each other and to the traditions of the sport. At the start of each match, they perform a ritual called peşrev. This ritual involves a series of movements and gestures that show their readiness and respect for the competition.

The history of yağlı güreş is deeply intertwined with Turkish culture. It has been depicted in various forms of art, including paintings and literature. This sport has also played a role in community bonding and has been a source of pride and identity for many regions in Turkey.

In recent years, yağlı güreş has gained international attention. While it remains a predominantly Turkish sport, efforts have been made to promote it globally. International competitions and exhibitions have been held, helping to introduce this unique form of wrestling to a wider audience.

The role of the olive oil in yağlı güreş goes beyond making the sport more challenging. Olive oil is a symbol of health and vitality in Turkish culture. It is also believed to have protective properties. The use of olive oil in the sport highlights its cultural significance and adds to the traditional aspect of the competition.

The Kırkpınar tournament is the highlight of the yağlı güreş calendar. It attracts wrestlers and spectators from all over Turkey and beyond. The event lasts for a week and includes various cultural activities alongside the wrestling matches. It is a celebration of Turkish heritage and the enduring spirit of this ancient sport.

Becoming a champion in yağlı güreş, or Başpehlivan, is a prestigious achievement. Champions earn respect and admiration within their communities. The title of Başpehlivan is not only a recognition of skill and strength but also of character and dedication to the sport.

Despite the challenges and physical demands, many wrestlers are deeply passionate about yağlı güreş. For them, it is more than just a sport; it is a way of life. The bonds formed through this shared passion often last a lifetime, creating a strong sense of camaraderie among the wrestlers.

The future of yağlı güreş looks promising. With continued efforts to preserve and promote the sport, it is likely to remain a cherished tradition in Turkey. Moreover, the growing international interest suggests that more people around the world will come to appreciate and participate in this unique form of wrestling.

In conclusion, yağlı güreş is a sport that combines physical prowess, cultural tradition, and a deep sense of respect. Its unique characteristics make it a fascinating and challenging sport. The enduring popularity of yağlı güreş is a testament to its significance in Turkish culture and its potential to captivate audiences around the world.

Historical Origins

The historical origins of yağlı güreş, also known as oil wrestling, can be traced back to ancient times. It is believed to have originated in the early days of the Ottoman Empire. Some historians suggest that the roots of this sport go even further back, possibly to ancient Greece and the Byzantine Empire. The exact beginnings are not clearly documented, but its long history is deeply embedded in Turkish culture.

In the early days, oil wrestling was more than just a sport. It was a way for warriors to train and demonstrate their strength and skills. The soldiers of the Ottoman Empire would engage in wrestling matches to prepare for battles. This training method helped them develop physical strength, agility, and combat techniques. Over time, these wrestling matches evolved into a popular form of entertainment and competition.

One of the earliest known references to oil wrestling comes from the 14th century. During this period, the Ottoman Empire was expanding its territory, and wrestling became a symbol of power and dominance. The sport was embraced by the ruling elite and became a part of military training and royal festivities.

It was during this time that the Kırkpınar tournament in Edirne began, which is now considered the oldest running sports event in the world.

The Kırkpınar tournament has a legendary origin story. According to tradition, the tournament started when 40 Ottoman soldiers engaged in a wrestling match during a break in their campaign. The match continued for hours until two soldiers wrestled into the night. Eventually, both men died from exhaustion, and they were buried under a fig tree. The following year, their comrades returned to the site to honor them, and thus the annual Kırkpınar festival began. This story, though possibly embellished over time, highlights the deep cultural and historical significance of the sport.

Throughout the Ottoman period, oil wrestling continued to grow in popularity. It was not only a military practice but also a civilian pastime. Local communities would organize wrestling matches during festivals and celebrations. These events were occasions for social gathering, entertainment, and showcasing local talent. The sport transcended social classes, with both commoners and nobility participating and attending the events.

During the 16th and 17th centuries, the Ottoman Empire was at its peak, and oil wrestling was firmly established as a national sport. Wrestlers, known as pehlivans, were highly respected and often received patronage from the sultans and other high-ranking officials. They were celebrated for their strength, skill, and sportsmanship. The pehlivans were not just athletes; they were cultural icons and heroes of their time.

The techniques and traditions of oil wrestling were passed down through generations. Fathers taught their sons, and local wrestling clubs, known as tekke, became centers for training and preserving the sport. These clubs were more than just places to learn wrestling; they were community hubs where values such as respect, honor, and discipline were instilled. The traditions and rituals associated with oil wrestling, like the peşrev (pre-match ritual), have been maintained through these local institutions.

In the 19th century, as the Ottoman Empire faced decline and modernization, oil wrestling remained a symbol of cultural identity and heritage. Despite the changes and challenges of the time, the sport continued to be a popular and important part of Turkish life. The Kırkpınar tournament and other regional competitions kept the tradition alive. The preservation of these events helped maintain a sense of continuity and connection to the past.

The 20th century brought significant changes to Turkey, including the establishment of the Republic of Turkey in 1923. During this period of transformation, many traditional practices were at risk of being lost. However, oil wrestling managed to survive and even thrive. The government recognized the cultural importance of the sport and took steps to preserve it. Efforts were made to organize official competitions, support local wrestling clubs, and promote the sport both nationally and internationally.

Oil wrestling's survival through the centuries is a testament to its deep-rooted significance in Turkish culture. The sport has managed to retain its traditional elements while adapting to modern times. Today, it is celebrated not only for its physical and competitive aspects but also for its cultural and historical importance. The annual Kırkpınar tournament remains a major event, attracting participants and spectators from around the world. It is a vibrant celebration of Turkish heritage, showcasing the enduring appeal of yağlı güreş.

In contemporary Turkey, oil wrestling continues to be a popular and respected sport. It is practiced by people of all ages, and local competitions are held throughout the country. The sport is also gaining recognition internationally, with efforts to introduce it to a broader audience. International exhibitions and competitions have been organized, highlighting the unique and challenging nature of oil wrestling.

The historical origins of oil wrestling are a rich tapestry of tradition, culture, and athleticism. From its beginnings in the early Ottoman Empire to its current status as a celebrated national sport, yağlı güreş has evolved while maintaining its core values and rituals. The sport's resilience and adaptability have ensured its place in the cultural heritage of Turkey. The ongoing efforts to preserve and promote oil wrestling are a reflection of its enduring significance and the pride that it instills in those who participate and witness it.

As oil wrestling moves into the future, it carries with it the weight of centuries of history. The sport's continued popularity and the dedication of its practitioners suggest that it will remain a vital part of Turkish culture for generations to come. The story of yağlı güreş is one of tradition, resilience, and the timeless appeal of human strength and skill.

Cultural Significance

Yağlı güreş, or oil wrestling, holds a unique place in Turkish culture. It is not just a sport but a rich tradition with deep cultural roots. This traditional sport is a symbol of strength, skill, and heritage. The cultural significance of yağlı güreş is profound and multifaceted, reflecting various aspects of Turkish society and history.

One of the key elements of oil wrestling's cultural significance is its role in preserving Turkish traditions. The sport has been practiced for centuries, maintaining rituals and customs that date back to the Ottoman Empire. These traditions are passed down through generations, ensuring that the cultural heritage associated with yağlı güreş is kept alive. The preservation of these rituals highlights the importance of continuity and respect for the past in Turkish culture.

Oil wrestling also plays a significant role in community bonding. Local communities often organize wrestling matches during festivals and celebrations. These events bring people together, fostering a sense of unity and shared identity. The communal aspect of yağlı güreş is evident in the way people gather to watch and support the wrestlers. This collective participation strengthens community ties and reinforces a sense of belonging.

The sport is also a celebration of physical prowess and skill. Wrestlers, known as pehlivans, are admired for their strength, agility, and technique. They undergo rigorous training to prepare for matches, and their dedication to the sport is highly respected. The admiration for pehlivans goes beyond their physical abilities; it extends to their discipline, perseverance, and sportsmanship. This respect for the athletes underscores the value placed on hard work and excellence in Turkish culture.

The use of olive oil in yağlı güreş has cultural and symbolic meanings. Olive oil is a significant element in Turkish cuisine and daily life, symbolizing health and vitality. In the context of oil wrestling, it represents purity and the sacredness of the competition. The tradition of dousing wrestlers in olive oil before matches adds a ritualistic aspect to the sport, emphasizing the spiritual and cultural dimensions of the practice.

The annual Kırkpınar tournament is a major cultural event in Turkey. It is not just a sports competition but a festival that includes various cultural activities. The tournament attracts thousands of spectators from all over the country and beyond. It is a time for celebration, where people come together to honor tradition and enjoy the festivities. The Kırkpınar tournament showcases the cultural richness of Turkey and highlights the enduring popularity of oil wrestling.

Oil wrestling is also a source of national pride. It is considered a uniquely Turkish sport, and its long history is a testament to the country's rich cultural heritage. The international recognition of yağlı güreş has further bolstered this sense of pride. Efforts to promote the sport globally have introduced it to new audiences, enhancing its cultural significance and reinforcing Turkey's identity on the world stage.

The sport's emphasis on respect and sportsmanship reflects important cultural values. Wrestlers show respect for their opponents, the referees, and the traditions of the sport. This respect is evident in the pre-match ritual known as peşrev, where wrestlers perform a series of movements and gestures to demonstrate their readiness and honor the competition. The emphasis on respect and fair play highlights the moral and ethical dimensions of yağlı güreş.

Oil wrestling also has a significant role in the cultural education of young people. Many children and young adults learn the sport from an early age, often training in local wrestling clubs. These clubs are not just places for physical training; they are centers for cultural learning and character development. Young wrestlers are taught the history, traditions, and values associated with the sport, fostering a deep appreciation for their cultural heritage.

The attire worn by wrestlers, particularly the leather trousers known as kıspet, has cultural significance. These trousers are handmade and crafted with care, symbolizing the skill and craftsmanship of Turkish artisans. The kıspet is more than just functional attire; it is a cultural artifact that connects wrestlers to the historical and traditional aspects of the sport. The care and pride taken in making and wearing the kıspet reflect the cultural importance of attention to detail and respect for tradition.

The cultural significance of oil wrestling extends to its depiction in art and literature. Throughout history, yağlı güreş has been portrayed in various forms of artistic expression. Paintings, poems, and stories celebrate the sport and its heroes, capturing the spirit and essence of the practice. These artistic representations contribute to the cultural narrative of oil wrestling, immortalizing its role in Turkish culture and history.

The sport also provides a platform for regional pride and identity. Different regions in Turkey have their own wrestling traditions and styles, adding to the diversity and richness of the sport. Local competitions and festivals allow regions to showcase their unique customs and talents. This regional variation highlights the cultural diversity within Turkey and the shared appreciation for oil wrestling across different communities.

In addition to its cultural significance, oil wrestling has economic implications. The Kırkpınar tournament and other major competitions attract tourists and generate revenue for local economies. The influx of visitors during these events provides economic benefits to host communities, supporting businesses and creating opportunities for local artisans and vendors. The economic impact of yağlı güreş underscores its broader significance beyond the cultural realm.

The ongoing efforts to preserve and promote oil wrestling are a reflection of its cultural importance. Various organizations and institutions are dedicated to maintaining the traditions and practices associated with the sport. These efforts include organizing competitions, supporting training programs, and promoting awareness of yağlı güreş both nationally and internationally. The commitment to preserving the sport highlights its enduring value and the desire to keep this cultural heritage alive for future generations.

Oil wrestling's cultural significance is also evident in its role in fostering international connections. While it remains a predominantly Turkish sport, international exhibitions and competitions have introduced it to a global audience. These events promote cultural exchange and understanding, showcasing the uniqueness of yağlı güreş and its place in the world of traditional sports. The international interest in oil wrestling reflects its universal appeal and the potential for cultural bridging.

The enduring popularity of oil wrestling is a testament to its deep cultural roots and significance. The sport's ability to adapt and thrive over centuries is a reflection of its resilience and the strong cultural values it embodies. As a symbol of Turkish heritage, oil wrestling continues to inspire and unite people, preserving a rich tradition while embracing modernity. The cultural significance of yağlı güreş lies in its role as a living tradition that connects the past, present, and future of Turkish culture.

The Wrestling Season

The wrestling season for yağlı güreş, or oil wrestling, follows a traditional and structured timeline. The season usually begins in the spring and continues through the summer months. This timing aligns with favorable weather conditions, allowing the matches to take place outdoors on grassy fields. The start of the season is marked by local festivals and small competitions, gradually building up to larger and more prestigious events.

At the beginning of the season, wrestlers start their intensive training programs. Training for oil wrestling is rigorous and demanding, focusing on building strength, endurance, and technique. Wrestlers, known as pehlivans, train daily to prepare for the upcoming competitions. Their training includes various exercises, practicing wrestling moves, and honing their skills. The commitment to training is a crucial aspect of a wrestler's preparation.

As the season progresses, local and regional competitions are held. These events are important for wrestlers to gain experience and improve their rankings. Local competitions are often community events, drawing spectators from the surrounding areas. They provide a platform for emerging talent to showcase their abilities and for seasoned wrestlers to maintain their competitive edge. These matches are also opportunities for the community to come together and celebrate their local traditions.

In the midst of the season, several major tournaments take place. These tournaments attract the best wrestlers from across the country. The matches become more intense and competitive as the stakes are higher. Winning a major tournament brings not only prestige but also significant rewards. The wrestlers strive to perform their best, knowing that their success in these tournaments can elevate their status in the wrestling community.

One of the most significant events in the wrestling season is the Kırkpınar tournament. This tournament, held annually in Edirne, is the highlight of the yağlı güreş calendar. It is the oldest running sports competition in the world, with a history spanning over 650 years. Wrestlers from all over Turkey and beyond come to compete in this prestigious event. The Kırkpınar tournament is a week-long celebration that includes various cultural activities alongside the wrestling matches.

The Kırkpınar tournament begins with an elaborate opening ceremony. This ceremony includes traditional music, dance, and other cultural performances. The wrestlers parade into the field, showcasing their readiness for the competition. The atmosphere is festive, with spectators eagerly anticipating the matches. The opening ceremony sets the tone for the tournament, highlighting the cultural richness of the event.

During the tournament, the matches are conducted with great ceremony and respect for tradition. Wrestlers start by dousing themselves in olive oil, making it challenging for their opponents to gain a grip. The matches are intense and physically demanding, requiring both strength and strategy. The wrestlers' skills are put to the test as they try to outmaneuver and overpower their opponents. Each match is a display of athleticism, technique, and endurance.

The climax of the Kırkpınar tournament is the final match, where the top wrestlers compete for the title of Başpehlivan, or chief wrestler. Winning this title is the highest honor in oil wrestling. The champion receives a golden belt and earns widespread recognition and respect. The final match is a highly anticipated event, drawing large crowds and significant media attention. It is a moment of glory for the winner and a testament to their dedication and skill.

After the Kırkpınar tournament, the wrestling season continues with other regional and national competitions. These events maintain the momentum of the season, allowing wrestlers to continue competing and improving. Each match contributes to the wrestlers' overall ranking and reputation. The season provides numerous opportunities for wrestlers to prove themselves and achieve their goals.

As the season comes to a close, the final competitions take place. These matches are often held in the autumn, marking the end of the wrestling season. Wrestlers give their best performances, aiming to finish the season on a high note. The end of the season is a time for reflection and evaluation. Wrestlers and their coaches review their performances, identifying areas for improvement and setting goals for the next season.

The wrestling season is not only about competition but also about camaraderie and tradition. Wrestlers form strong bonds with each other, sharing a sense of brotherhood and mutual respect. The season fosters a sense of community among the wrestlers, coaches, and supporters. This camaraderie is a vital part of the sport, creating a supportive and encouraging environment.

Throughout the season, the role of the trainers and coaches is crucial. They guide the wrestlers in their training, offering advice and support. Coaches help wrestlers develop their techniques, improve their strategies, and maintain their physical condition. The relationship between a wrestler and their coach is built on trust and respect, contributing significantly to the wrestler's success.

The wrestling season is also a time for cultural celebration. Each competition and tournament is accompanied by various cultural activities, showcasing Turkish traditions and heritage. These activities include music, dance, and food, providing a festive atmosphere. The cultural aspect of the wrestling season adds depth and richness to the sport, highlighting its importance in Turkish culture.

The season's end is marked by ceremonies and celebrations. Wrestlers are honored for their achievements, and the champions receive their awards. These ceremonies are a time for recognition and appreciation, celebrating the hard work and dedication of the wrestlers. The end of the season is a culmination of months of effort and competition, bringing a sense of accomplishment and fulfillment.

After the season ends, wrestlers take a period of rest and recovery. This time is essential for healing and rejuvenating their bodies. The off-season allows wrestlers to relax and spend time with their families. It is also a time for planning and preparation for the next season. Wrestlers set new goals and start thinking about their training programs, looking forward to another year of competition.

The wrestling season for yağlı güreş is a dynamic and multifaceted journey. It encompasses rigorous training, intense competition, cultural celebration, and personal growth. The season is a testament to the dedication and passion of the wrestlers, coaches, and supporters. It reflects the deep cultural significance of oil wrestling in Turkish society. The wrestling season is a vibrant and integral part of the sport, highlighting the enduring appeal and tradition of yağlı güreş.

Yağlı güreş, or oil wrestling, is steeped in rituals and traditions that are integral to the sport. These practices have been passed down through generations, preserving the cultural heritage of Turkish oil wrestling. Each ritual and tradition carries deep significance, adding layers of meaning to the competition.

One of the most important rituals in oil wrestling is the preparation of the wrestlers. Before a match, wrestlers cover their bodies with olive oil. This practice serves multiple purposes. It makes it difficult for opponents to gain a firm grip, increasing the challenge of the match. Additionally, olive oil holds cultural and symbolic value. It represents purity, health, and vitality, and its use in wrestling connects the sport to these positive attributes.

The kıspet, the leather trousers worn by wrestlers, is another key tradition. These trousers are handmade and crafted with care. The process of making kıspet involves skilled artisans who use high-quality leather. Wrestlers take great pride in their kıspet, which are not just functional attire but also symbols of their identity and connection to the sport's history. The kıspet is designed to withstand the rigors of oil wrestling, providing durability and comfort.

The peşrev is a pre-match ritual that wrestlers perform before the actual competition begins. This ritual involves a series of movements and gestures that show respect and readiness for the match. Wrestlers walk around the field, clapping their hands and performing specific motions. The peşrev is not just a physical warm-up; it is a ceremonial act that honors the tradition of oil wrestling. It sets the tone for the match, emphasizing respect, honor, and sportsmanship.

Another significant tradition is the prayer or dua that wrestlers say before the match. This prayer seeks blessings for a fair and honorable competition. Wrestlers ask for strength, protection, and fairness. The prayer reflects the spiritual dimension of oil wrestling, acknowledging the role of faith and divine support in the sport. This ritual underscores the moral and ethical values that are central to yağlı güreş.

The match itself is conducted with a deep sense of tradition. Wrestlers engage in various techniques and strategies to overpower their opponents. The goal is to either pin the opponent's back to the ground or lift and carry them for a certain distance. The techniques used in oil wrestling are unique and require skill and practice. Wrestlers rely on their training, strength, and agility to succeed. The conduct of the match is governed by rules and traditions that ensure fairness and respect.

One of the unique aspects of oil wrestling is the absence of a fixed time limit for matches. This tradition allows matches to continue until a clear winner emerges. The length of a match can vary, sometimes lasting for several hours. This open-ended nature adds to the physical and mental challenge of the sport. Wrestlers must maintain their stamina and focus throughout the match, demonstrating endurance and perseverance.

The role of the cazgır, or announcer, is another important tradition in oil wrestling. The cazgır introduces the wrestlers and provides commentary during the match. Their announcements are often poetic and rhythmic, adding a ceremonial flair to the event. The cazgır's role is not just to inform but also to entertain and engage the audience. This tradition enhances the atmosphere of the match, creating a lively and dynamic experience for spectators.

After a match, the victor performs a traditional victory dance. This dance is a celebratory ritual that showcases the wrestler's joy and pride. The dance is often accompanied by music and applause from the audience. The victory dance is a moment of personal and communal celebration, highlighting the significance of the win. It is a time for the wrestler to bask in their achievement and for the community to share in their triumph.

The Kırkpınar tournament, the most prestigious event in oil wrestling, is rich with traditions. The tournament begins with an elaborate opening ceremony that includes music, dance, and cultural performances. Wrestlers parade into the field, and the atmosphere is festive. The opening ceremony is a grand spectacle that sets the stage for the competition. It is a celebration of Turkish culture and the enduring tradition of oil wrestling.

Throughout the Kırkpınar tournament, various cultural activities take place alongside the wrestling matches. These activities include traditional Turkish music, folk dances, and exhibitions of local crafts and cuisine. The festival atmosphere of the tournament highlights the cultural richness of the event. It is a time for people to come together, enjoy the festivities, and celebrate their shared heritage.

The awarding of the golden belt to the Başpehlivan, or chief wrestler, is a significant tradition. The golden belt is a symbol of the highest honor in oil wrestling. It is awarded to the champion of the Kırkpınar tournament. This tradition dates back centuries and is a prestigious achievement. The golden belt represents excellence, dedication, and the pinnacle of success in the sport. Winning the belt is a moment of great pride for the wrestler and their community.

The tradition of passing down techniques and knowledge from one generation to the next is fundamental to oil wrestling. Experienced wrestlers mentor younger ones, teaching them the skills and values of the sport. This mentorship ensures the continuity of the tradition and the preservation of its core principles. The relationship between mentors and mentees is built on respect and trust, fostering a sense of community and shared purpose.

The role of the wrestling clubs, or tekkes, is also crucial. These clubs are centers for training and cultural learning. They provide a space for wrestlers to practice, train, and develop their skills. The tekkes are also places where the traditions and values of oil wrestling are upheld and passed on. The sense of community within these clubs is strong, creating bonds among wrestlers and supporting their growth and development.

The end-of-season celebrations and ceremonies are important traditions in oil wrestling. These events honor the achievements of the wrestlers and celebrate the conclusion of the wrestling season. Wrestlers are recognized for their performances, and awards are given. The ceremonies are a time for reflection and appreciation, acknowledging the hard work and dedication of the wrestlers. It is a moment to look back on the season and celebrate the collective efforts of the wrestling community.

The preservation of oil wrestling's rituals and traditions is a collective effort. Various organizations and institutions are dedicated to maintaining these practices. They organize competitions, support training programs, and promote awareness of the sport. These efforts ensure that the rich cultural heritage of oil wrestling is preserved for future generations. The commitment to these traditions reflects their importance in Turkish culture and the desire to keep them alive.

The rituals and traditions of oil wrestling are a testament to the sport's deep cultural roots. They add meaning and depth to the competition, creating a rich and vibrant experience for both participants and spectators. These practices connect the present to the past, honoring the history and heritage of yağlı güreş. The continued observance of these traditions ensures that the sport remains a living and dynamic part of Turkish culture.

The respect for tradition in oil wrestling is a reflection of broader cultural values. It emphasizes the importance of heritage, community, and continuity. The rituals and traditions of the sport highlight the balance between maintaining the past and embracing the present. This balance is a key aspect of the cultural significance of yağlı güreş, ensuring its enduring appeal and relevance.

Oil wrestling's key rituals and traditions are integral to its identity. They enrich the sport, providing structure, meaning, and cultural depth. The observance of these practices reflects a deep respect for history and tradition, ensuring that oil wrestling remains a cherished and celebrated part of Turkish culture. The rituals and traditions of yağlı güreş are not just customs; they are the heart and soul of the sport.

Yağlı güreş, or oil wrestling, is celebrated through various iconic tournaments and festivals. These events are integral to the sport, showcasing the skill and tradition of oil wrestling. Each tournament and festival has its unique characteristics, attracting wrestlers and spectators from all over.

The most famous and prestigious of these events is the Kırkpınar tournament. Held annually in Edirne,

Turkey, this tournament is the oldest running sports competition in the world, with a history spanning over 650 years. The Kırkpınar tournament is a week-long event that includes wrestling matches, cultural activities, and various festivities. Wrestlers from across Turkey and beyond come to compete for the title of Başpehlivan, or chief wrestler. Winning the Kırkpınar tournament is the highest honor in oil wrestling.

The Kırkpınar tournament begins with an elaborate opening ceremony. This ceremony includes traditional music, dance, and other cultural performances. Wrestlers parade into the field, showcasing their readiness for the competition. The festive atmosphere draws large crowds, creating an exciting and vibrant start to the tournament. The opening ceremony sets the tone for the entire event, emphasizing the cultural richness and historical significance of the Kırkpınar tournament.

Throughout the Kırkpınar tournament, matches are held in a highly ceremonial manner. Wrestlers cover themselves in olive oil and wear leather trousers called kıspet. The matches are intense and physically demanding, requiring both strength and strategy. The rules are simple but challenging, with the goal being to pin the opponent's back to the ground or lift and carry them for a certain distance. Each match is a test of endurance, skill, and mental fortitude.

Another iconic tournament is the Elmalı Oil Wrestling Festival, held in the town of Elmalı in Antalya Province. This festival is one of the oldest in Turkey, with a history dating back to the 14th century. The Elmalı festival is known for its vibrant atmosphere and strong community involvement. Like the Kırkpınar tournament, it features traditional music, dance, and other cultural activities. The Elmalı festival is a major event in the region, drawing participants and spectators from near and far.

The Elmalı Oil Wrestling Festival includes various age categories, allowing wrestlers of all ages to compete. This inclusiveness fosters a sense of community and encourages the participation of younger generations. The matches are conducted with the same respect for tradition and ritual seen in other oil wrestling events. The Elmalı festival is a celebration of Turkish heritage, showcasing the enduring appeal of yağlı güreş.

The Seyitgazi Oil Wrestling Festival is another important event in the oil wrestling calendar. Held in the town of Seyitgazi in Eskişehir Province, this festival honors Seyit Battal Gazi, a legendary Islamic warrior. The festival includes wrestling matches, religious ceremonies, and other cultural activities. The Seyitgazi festival is unique in its combination of sport and spiritual observance, highlighting the deep cultural and historical connections of oil wrestling.

The Seyitgazi festival attracts wrestlers from various regions, contributing to a diverse and competitive field. The matches are conducted with great ceremony and respect for tradition. Wrestlers and spectators alike participate in the religious and cultural aspects of the festival, creating a multifaceted celebration. The Seyitgazi Oil Wrestling Festival is a testament to the rich cultural tapestry of Turkey and the integral role of oil wrestling within it.

The Kocaeli Oil Wrestling Festival is another significant event. Held in the Kocaeli Province, this festival is known for its large-scale organization and high level of competition. The Kocaeli festival includes matches in various weight categories, providing opportunities for wrestlers of different sizes and skill levels. The event also features traditional music, dance, and other cultural activities, adding to its festive atmosphere.

The Kocaeli Oil Wrestling Festival is an important platform for emerging talent. Many young wrestlers use this festival to showcase their skills and gain recognition. The matches are intense and competitive, reflecting the high standards of the event. The Kocaeli festival is a key part of the oil wrestling season, contributing to the sport's popularity and cultural significance.

The Sarayiçi Oil Wrestling Festival, held in Edirne, is closely associated with the Kırkpınar tournament. This festival is part of the larger Kırkpınar event, taking place in the historic Sarayiçi area. The Sarayiçi festival includes preliminary matches and cultural activities, setting the stage for the main Kırkpınar tournament. The Sarayiçi festival is a vibrant celebration of oil wrestling and Turkish heritage, drawing large crowds and media attention.

The Kaş Oil Wrestling Festival, held in the town of Kaş in Antalya Province, is another notable event. This festival is known for its picturesque setting and strong community involvement. The Kaş festival includes wrestling matches, traditional music, and other cultural activities. The matches are conducted with respect for tradition and ritual, showcasing the skill and dedication of the wrestlers. The Kaş festival is a beloved event in the region, attracting participants and spectators from all over.

The Kumluca Oil Wrestling Festival, also held in Antalya Province, is a major event in the oil wrestling calendar. This festival is known for its large-scale organization and competitive matches. The Kumluca festival includes various weight categories, allowing for a diverse field of wrestlers. The event also features traditional music, dance, and other cultural activities, creating a festive atmosphere. The Kumluca festival is an important platform for wrestlers to demonstrate their skills and gain recognition.

The Altınova Oil Wrestling Festival, held in the Yalova Province, is another significant event. This festival is known for its strong community involvement and vibrant atmosphere. The Altınova festival includes wrestling matches, traditional music, and other cultural activities. The matches are conducted with respect for tradition and ritual, reflecting the deep cultural significance of oil wrestling. The Altınova festival is a celebration of Turkish heritage and the enduring appeal of yağlı güreş.

The Edirne Oil Wrestling Festival, distinct from the Kırkpınar tournament but held in the same region, is another important event. This festival includes matches and cultural activities that highlight the rich history of oil wrestling in Edirne. The Edirne festival is a major event in the region, attracting wrestlers and spectators from all over. The matches are conducted with great ceremony and respect for tradition, showcasing the skill and dedication of the participants.

The iconic tournaments and festivals of yağlı güreş are integral to the sport's identity and cultural significance. These events provide a platform for wrestlers to showcase their skills and for communities to celebrate their heritage. Each festival and tournament has its unique characteristics, contributing to the rich tapestry of Turkish oil wrestling. The continued popularity and success of these events reflect the enduring appeal and cultural importance of yağlı güreş.

Two Notable Wrestlers

In the world of yağlı güreş, or oil wrestling, there have been many notable wrestlers who have made significant contributions to the sport. Two such wrestlers are Kel Aliço and Ahmet Taşçı. Their achievements and legacies have left an indelible mark on the history of oil wrestling.

Kel Aliço, also known as "Bald Aliço," was born in 1845 in the village of Dereköy, in the Edirne Province of the Ottoman Empire. His nickname, "Kel," means bald, a characteristic that became part of his identity. Kel Aliço began his wrestling career at a young age, quickly demonstrating exceptional skill and strength. His prowess in oil wrestling soon earned him a reputation as one of the most formidable wrestlers of his time.

Kel Aliço's wrestling style was characterized by his incredible strength and endurance. He was known for his ability to outlast his opponents, often winning matches that lasted for hours. His technique was a combination of brute force and strategic maneuvers, allowing him to dominate the wrestling field. Kel Aliço's matches were highly anticipated events, drawing large crowds who were eager to witness his remarkable performances.

One of Kel Aliço's most significant achievements was his long reign as the Başpehlivan, or chief wrestler, at the Kırkpınar tournament. He held this title for an unprecedented 27 years, from 1861 to 1888. This remarkable record remains unbroken and is a testament to his extraordinary skill and dedication. Kel Aliço's dominance at Kırkpınar solidified his status as a legend in the sport of oil wrestling.

Kel Aliço's influence extended beyond his wrestling matches. He was a mentor to many young wrestlers, passing down his techniques and knowledge. His guidance helped shape the next generation of wrestlers, ensuring the continuity of the sport's traditions. Kel Aliço's legacy as both a champion and a mentor has left a lasting impact on the world of yağlı güreş.

Ahmet Taşçı, another notable wrestler, was born in 1958 in the town of Karamürsel, in Kocaeli Province, Turkey. Ahmet Taşçı began his wrestling career in the 1970s, quickly rising through the ranks with his exceptional skill and determination. He became known for his powerful and aggressive wrestling style, which set him apart from his peers.

Ahmet Taşçı's career was marked by numerous victories and titles. He won the prestigious Kırkpınar tournament nine times, earning the title of Başpehlivan. His first victory at Kırkpınar came in 1985, and he continued to dominate the tournament throughout the late 1980s and 1990s. Ahmet Taşçı's success at Kırkpınar made him one of the most celebrated wrestlers in the history of oil wrestling.

Ahmet Taşçı's wrestling style was a blend of strength, speed, and technique. He was known for his quick movements and powerful holds, which often left his opponents struggling to keep up. His ability to adapt to different opponents and situations made him a formidable competitor. Ahmet Taşçı's matches were thrilling spectacles, captivating audiences with his dynamic performances.

In addition to his success at Kırkpınar, Ahmet Taşçı achieved international recognition. He participated in various international oil wrestling competitions, showcasing his talent on a global stage. His participation in these events helped promote the sport of yağlı güreş beyond Turkey's borders, contributing to its growing popularity worldwide.

Ahmet Taşçı's contributions to oil wrestling extended beyond his achievements in the ring. He was dedicated to promoting the sport and its traditions. He worked as a coach and mentor, training young wrestlers and helping them develop their skills. Ahmet Taşçı's commitment to nurturing new talent ensured the continued growth and vitality of yağlı güreş.

Both Kel Aliço and Ahmet Taşçı have left enduring legacies in the world of oil wrestling. Their exceptional skills, numerous victories, and dedication to the sport have made them iconic figures. They have inspired generations of wrestlers and fans, contributing to the rich history and cultural significance of yağlı güreş.

The stories of Kel Aliço and Ahmet Taşçı highlight the importance of dedication, skill, and tradition in oil wrestling. Their careers serve as examples of how hard work and passion can lead to extraordinary achievements. These wrestlers have not only set records but also shaped the sport, ensuring its continued relevance and appeal.

Kel Aliço and Ahmet Taşçı are remembered not only for their victories but also for their contributions to the community of wrestlers. Their roles as mentors and coaches have helped maintain the traditions and values of oil wrestling. By passing on their knowledge and expertise, they have ensured that future generations can continue to enjoy and participate in this unique sport.

The impact of Kel Aliço and Ahmet Taşçı extends beyond the wrestling field. They are cultural icons whose stories reflect the broader history and heritage of Turkey. Their achievements in oil wrestling are a source of national pride, highlighting the strength and resilience of Turkish culture. The legacies of these wrestlers are celebrated in festivals, tournaments, and cultural events, keeping their memory alive.

The lives and careers of Kel Aliço and Ahmet Taşçı illustrate the deep connection between oil wrestling and Turkish culture. Their dedication to the sport and its traditions exemplifies the values of respect, honor, and perseverance that are central to yağlı güreş. These wrestlers have become symbols of the sport's enduring legacy and cultural significance.

The stories of Kel Aliço and Ahmet Taşçı continue to inspire new generations of wrestlers. Their achievements and contributions to oil wrestling serve as a benchmark for aspiring wrestlers. The legacy of these iconic figures is a testament to the enduring appeal and cultural importance of yağlı güreş.

The enduring legacies of Kel Aliço and Ahmet Taşçı are a reminder of the rich history and cultural significance of oil wrestling. Their remarkable careers and contributions to the sport have left an indelible mark on the world of yağlı güreş. The stories of these wrestlers continue to inspire and captivate, highlighting the unique and timeless appeal of oil wrestling.

Training for yağlı güreş, or oil wrestling, is a rigorous and comprehensive process. It begins with building physical strength. Wrestlers engage in weight training to increase their muscle mass and power. This training includes lifting weights, doing push-ups, and performing other strength-building exercises. Developing physical strength is essential as it provides the foundation for the various techniques used in oil wrestling.

In addition to strength training, wrestlers work on their cardiovascular endurance. They run, swim, and engage in high-intensity interval training to improve their stamina. Cardiovascular fitness is crucial because matches can last for hours without a fixed time limit. Wrestlers need to maintain their energy levels and remain agile throughout the competition. This endurance training ensures they can perform at their best for extended periods.

Flexibility is another important aspect of training. Wrestlers stretch regularly to enhance their flexibility. This helps them execute the intricate moves required in oil wrestling. Being flexible allows wrestlers to maneuver their bodies more effectively, making it easier to escape holds and apply techniques. Stretching exercises include yoga, dynamic stretching, and other flexibility routines.

Technique training is a critical component of preparation. Wrestlers learn and practice various moves and holds specific to oil wrestling. These techniques include the arm lock, leg sweep, and body throw. Each move is practiced repeatedly to ensure precision and effectiveness. Wrestlers often train with partners to simulate match conditions, allowing them to refine their techniques in realistic scenarios.

Wrestlers also practice the ritualistic elements of oil wrestling. They learn the peşrev, the pre-match ritual, which involves a series of movements and gestures. This ritual is performed before each match to show respect and readiness. Practicing the peşrev helps wrestlers connect with the traditions of the sport and prepare mentally for the competition. It is an important part of their overall training regimen.

Mental preparation is a key aspect of training. Wrestlers engage in various mental exercises to build focus and resilience. Visualization techniques are commonly used, where wrestlers imagine themselves performing successfully in matches. This mental rehearsal helps them develop confidence and reduce anxiety. Meditation and breathing exercises are also practiced to enhance concentration and calmness.

Nutrition plays a vital role in a wrestler's training program. A balanced diet rich in proteins, carbohydrates, and healthy fats is essential for maintaining energy levels and supporting muscle growth. Wrestlers often work with nutritionists to create meal plans tailored to their needs. Proper hydration is also emphasized, as staying hydrated is crucial for optimal performance during training and matches.

Rest and recovery are integral to a wrestler's training regimen. After intense training sessions, wrestlers need time to recover and rebuild their muscles. This recovery period includes proper sleep, rest days, and activities like massage and physiotherapy. Taking care of their bodies ensures that wrestlers remain in peak physical condition and reduces the risk of injuries.

Sparring sessions are a significant part of training. During these sessions, wrestlers practice their techniques in simulated match conditions. Sparring helps them apply what they have learned in real-time and develop their strategy. It also allows them to experience the physical and mental demands of a match, preparing them for the actual competition. Coaches provide feedback and guidance during these sessions to help wrestlers improve.

Coaching is an essential element of training. Coaches are experienced wrestlers who provide instruction, support, and motivation. They help wrestlers develop their techniques, refine their strategies, and improve their overall performance. The relationship between a wrestler and their coach is built on trust and respect. Coaches play a critical role in a wrestler's development and success.

Wrestlers also engage in off-season training to maintain their fitness and skills. The off-season is a time for focusing on general physical conditioning and refining techniques. Wrestlers use this period to address any weaknesses and prepare for the upcoming season. Off-season training ensures that wrestlers stay in shape and are ready to start the new season at their best.

Competition experience is a vital part of a wrestler's training journey. Participating in local and regional competitions helps wrestlers gain valuable experience. These matches allow them to test their skills, learn from their mistakes, and build their confidence. The experience gained from competing is crucial for their development and preparation for major tournaments.

The training environment is also important. Many wrestlers train in wrestling clubs, known as tekkes. These clubs provide the facilities and resources needed for effective training. They also foster a sense of community among wrestlers. Training in a supportive environment helps wrestlers stay motivated and focused. The camaraderie within these clubs enhances their overall training experience.

Family support plays a significant role in a wrestler's training. Many wrestlers come from families with a strong tradition of oil wrestling. This familial support provides encouragement and motivation. Family members often play active roles in a wrestler's training and preparation, helping them stay committed to their goals. The support system within the family is a crucial aspect of a wrestler's journey.

Peer support is another important factor. Wrestlers train alongside their peers, who share similar goals and challenges. This peer group provides a source of motivation and accountability. Training with peers creates a competitive yet supportive environment, pushing wrestlers to perform at their best. The bonds formed with fellow wrestlers are an important part of the training experience.

Community involvement is a significant aspect of training. Local communities often support their wrestlers by attending matches and providing encouragement. This community support creates a sense of pride and responsibility in the wrestlers. Knowing that they have the backing of their community motivates them to train harder and perform well. The connection with the community is a source of inspiration.

The historical and cultural significance of oil wrestling is emphasized during training. Wrestlers are taught the history and traditions of the sport. This knowledge instills a sense of pride and respect for the heritage of yağlı güreş. Understanding the cultural context of the sport helps wrestlers appreciate their role in preserving and continuing these traditions.

Training for yağlı güreş is a comprehensive and demanding process. It involves building physical strength, enhancing endurance, improving flexibility, and mastering techniques. Mental preparation, proper nutrition, and adequate rest are also crucial. Sparring sessions, coaching, and competition experience contribute to a wrestler's development. The supportive environment of wrestling clubs, family, peers, and the community plays a significant role. The emphasis on historical and cultural significance enriches the training experience. This holistic approach ensures that wrestlers are well-prepared for the challenges of oil wrestling.

Costumes and Gear

In yağlı güreş, or oil wrestling, the costumes and gear are essential elements that contribute to the sport's uniqueness. The main piece of attire is the kıspet, which are traditional leather trousers. These trousers are handmade from high-quality, durable leather. The process of making kıspet is intricate, requiring skilled craftsmanship. The leather used is usually from water buffalo or cowhide, chosen for its strength and flexibility.

Kıspet are designed to withstand the rigors of oil wrestling. The trousers cover the wrestler from the waist to just below the knees. They are fitted tightly to prevent opponents from easily grabbing hold. The tight fit is crucial because it minimizes the chances of the opponent gaining leverage. Kıspet are secured with strong leather straps around the waist and thighs, ensuring they stay in place during intense matches.

The leather for kıspet is treated and conditioned to make it soft and comfortable. This process involves soaking the leather in water and oil, then stretching and shaping it to the desired fit. The conditioning also helps the leather withstand the liberal application of olive oil during matches. Well-maintained kıspet can last for many years, serving as a valuable piece of gear for wrestlers.

Wrestlers often have a personal connection to their kıspet. These trousers are sometimes passed down from generation to generation, symbolizing the continuation of family traditions in oil wrestling. The kıspet are often customized to fit the individual wrestler perfectly, reflecting their personal style and preference. This customization adds to the sentimental value and importance of the kıspet.

Another essential piece of gear is the olive oil itself. Wrestlers apply copious amounts of olive oil to their bodies before and during matches. This oiling makes it extremely difficult for opponents to gain a firm grip, adding an extra layer of challenge to the sport. The olive oil used is usually high quality, ensuring it is safe and effective. Applying the oil is a ritualistic process, involving careful and thorough coverage of the entire body.

The oil application starts with the wrestler pouring oil onto their hands and then rubbing it over their body. They focus on covering the arms, chest, back, and legs. The process requires assistance, often from a coach or fellow wrestler, to ensure every part of the body is adequately oiled. This thorough application is essential to maintain the slipperiness that defines oil wrestling.

The gear also includes protective elements, such as kneepads and ankle supports. These items help prevent injuries during matches. Kneepads are often worn under the kıspet, providing cushioning and protection to the knees. Ankle supports help stabilize the ankles, reducing the risk of sprains and other injuries. While not always visible, these protective items are crucial for the wrestler's safety.

Wrestlers also use towels as part of their gear. Towels are used to wipe off excess oil and sweat during breaks in the match. They help maintain a manageable level of slipperiness, ensuring that the wrestlers can continue to grapple effectively. Towels are kept handy by coaches or assistants at the side of the wrestling field. These items are simple but vital for the wrestler's comfort and performance.

The traditional headgear worn by some wrestlers is known as a puşi. This cloth headgear serves both practical and symbolic purposes. Practically, it helps absorb sweat and keeps the wrestler's hair out of their face. Symbolically, it can represent the wrestler's region or wrestling club. The puşi adds a touch of tradition and identity to the wrestler's appearance.

Footwear is generally not used in oil wrestling. Wrestlers compete barefoot, which allows for better grip and balance on the grass or ground. Wrestling barefoot is also a tradition that dates back centuries. It connects wrestlers to the historical roots of the sport, maintaining the authenticity and simplicity of oil wrestling.

The gear used in training also includes mats and practice areas. These areas are designed to simulate the conditions of actual matches. Mats provide a safe and cushioned surface for practicing throws and holds. They are essential for preventing injuries during training. The practice areas are usually well-maintained to ensure a safe environment for wrestlers to hone their skills.

In addition to physical gear, wrestlers often have personal items that hold sentimental value. These can include lucky charms, talismans, or items given by family members. Such items are carried or worn discreetly, serving as sources of motivation and comfort. These personal items add a layer of emotional and psychological support for the wrestler.

The preparation and care of gear are crucial aspects of a wrestler's routine. Maintaining kıspet involves regular cleaning and conditioning of the leather. This care ensures the trousers remain supple and durable. Wrestlers and their coaches take great pride in the upkeep of their gear, as it reflects their dedication to the sport. Proper care extends the life of the gear, allowing it to perform well over time.

Olive oil storage is also an important consideration. The oil needs to be kept in clean, sealed containers to maintain its quality. Wrestlers ensure that their supply of olive oil is fresh and uncontaminated. Proper storage prevents the oil from going rancid, which could affect its effectiveness and safety. This attention to detail in gear maintenance is a testament to the professionalism and discipline of the wrestlers.

The gear used in oil wrestling is more than just functional; it is a part of the sport's identity and tradition. Each piece, from the kıspet to the olive oil, plays a vital role in the practice and performance of yağlı güreş. The careful selection, preparation, and maintenance of this gear reflect the wrestler's respect for the sport and its history. The unique combination of these elements creates the distinctive experience of oil wrestling.

Overall, the costumes and gear in oil wrestling are deeply intertwined with the sport's traditions and practices. They contribute to the distinctive nature of yağlı güreş, making it a unique and culturally rich form of wrestling. The attention to detail in the design, preparation, and maintenance of the gear underscores the dedication and passion of the wrestlers. Through these elements, oil wrestling continues to be a celebrated and respected sport.

In Yağlı Güreş, music and drumming play crucial roles. They're not just background noise but integral to the entire event. The music sets the rhythm and pace of the match. It starts slow, gradually building momentum as the wrestlers warm up. The drumming intensifies, mirroring the physical exertion and emotions of the wrestlers. It's synchronized with their movements, adding drama and energy to the spectacle.

The music isn't random; it follows traditional patterns that resonate with the audience. Each beat has a purpose, guiding both wrestlers and spectators through the stages of the match. It's like a conversation between the drummers and the wrestlers, where rhythm dictates action. The melodies are deeply rooted in Turkish culture, evoking pride and passion among those watching.

Drumming in Yağlı Güreş isn't just about sound; it's about tradition and heritage. The drummers themselves are revered for their skill and timing. They're like storytellers, using beats to narrate the struggle unfolding in the arena. Their instruments are sacred, passed down through generations, embodying the spirit of this ancient sport.

As the match progresses, the drumming reaches a crescendo, marking pivotal moments. It's not just about volume but about intensity. The beats quicken as wrestlers push themselves to the limit, capturing the raw emotion of victory and defeat. Audiences are swept up in the rhythm, feeling every twist and turn of the contest.

Music and drumming are also a form of communication in Yağlı Güreş. They convey respect, determination, and courage. Wrestlers draw strength from the music, using its cadence to time their moves. Even in the midst of physical combat, they remain attuned to the drumbeats, finding inspiration and resolve in their steady pulse.

In conclusion, music and drumming are inseparable from Yağlı Güreş. They're not mere accompaniments but essential components that elevate the sport to an art form. Through rhythm and melody, they connect wrestlers to their audience and to their cultural heritage. Yağlı Güreş isn't just about strength and skill; it's about tradition and passion, and music and drumming embody these values in every beat.

Modern Adaptations

Modern adaptations of Yağlı Güreş reflect changes in society and technology. These adaptations aren't just about updating the sport; they're about preserving its essence while making it relevant to contemporary audiences. One notable adaptation is the inclusion of electronic music alongside traditional drumming. This blend bridges the gap between old and new, appealing to younger generations while respecting the sport's roots.

Technology has also influenced the presentation of Yağlı Güreş. Matches are now live-streamed and broadcasted globally, reaching a wider audience than ever before. This exposure not only boosts the sport's popularity but also introduces it to new cultures and markets. Viewers can now experience the excitement of Yağlı Güreş from anywhere in the world, creating a global community of fans.

Another modern adaptation is the use of social media to promote and share Yağlı Güreş. Wrestlers and organizers leverage platforms like Instagram and YouTube to showcase matches, training sessions, and behind-the-scenes footage. This direct engagement with fans enhances their connection to the sport and builds anticipation for upcoming events.

Training methods have also evolved to incorporate modern sports science. Wrestlers now have access to advanced nutrition plans, fitness regimes, and recovery techniques. This scientific approach enhances their performance and reduces the risk of injury, ensuring they can compete at the highest level.

In addition to technological advancements, Yağlı Güreş has embraced inclusivity and diversity. Women's competitions have gained recognition, offering female wrestlers a platform to showcase their skills. This shift promotes gender equality within the sport and attracts a more diverse audience.

Furthermore, Yağlı Güreş has adapted its rules and regulations to ensure fairness and safety. Refereeing techniques have become more standardized, with officials trained to enforce rules consistently. This professionalism enhances the legitimacy of the sport and builds trust among participants and spectators alike.

In conclusion, modern adaptations have revitalized Yağlı Güreş for the 21st century. From technological innovations to inclusivity and professionalization, these changes have not only preserved its heritage but also secured its future. By embracing new ideas while honoring tradition, Yağlı Güreş continues to evolve, captivating audiences worldwide with its blend of athleticism, culture, and community.

International Influence

International influence has significantly impacted Yağlı Güreş, integrating it into the global sports landscape. Through cultural exchange and international competitions, Yağlı Güreş has gained recognition beyond Turkey's borders. Wrestlers from diverse backgrounds now participate, bringing their own techniques and styles to enrich the sport.

The spread of Yağlı Güreş internationally has fostered mutual understanding and appreciation among different cultures. Competitions serve as platforms for athletes to showcase their skills and build camaraderie with competitors from around the world. This exchange of ideas strengthens the global community of wrestlers and fans alike.

Furthermore, international tournaments promote tourism and cultural exchange. Host countries benefit economically from hosting events, attracting visitors who contribute to the local economy. This exposure also enhances the country's reputation as a hub for sports and cultural exchange.

Moreover, Yağlı Güreş's international presence has sparked interest in Turkish culture and traditions. Spectators and participants alike learn about Turkey's rich history through the sport, fostering a deeper appreciation for its heritage. This cultural exchange promotes tolerance and respect for diversity among global audiences.

Additionally, international recognition has spurred efforts to standardize rules and regulations. Organizations collaborate to establish guidelines that ensure fairness and consistency in competitions. This professionalism enhances the sport's credibility and attracts top talent from around the world.

In conclusion, international influence has transformed Yağlı Güreş into a global phenomenon. Through cultural exchange, economic benefits, and standardized regulations, the sport continues to grow in popularity and significance on the world stage. By embracing diversity and promoting mutual respect, Yağlı Güreş bridges cultures and unites communities through the universal language of sport.

Conclusion: *The Future of Yağlı Güreş*

The future of Yağlı Güreş holds promise and challenges as it evolves in the modern world. Embracing technological advancements will be crucial, with innovations in broadcasting and digital platforms enhancing global visibility. This connectivity allows more people to experience the sport, fostering a broader fan base and ensuring its continued relevance in the digital age.

Furthermore, preserving Yağlı Güreş's traditional values while adapting to contemporary demands is essential. This balance ensures that the sport remains rooted in its cultural heritage while appealing to new generations. By honoring its origins and rituals, Yağlı Güreş maintains authenticity and respect among participants and spectators alike.

Education and outreach programs will play a vital role in securing Yağlı Güreş's future. Introducing the sport to schools and communities fosters interest from a young age, nurturing future wrestlers and fans. These initiatives also promote values such as discipline, respect, and sportsmanship, contributing positively to society.

Moreover, sustainability practices are becoming increasingly important in sports. Yağlı Güreş can lead by example in promoting eco-friendly initiatives, from reducing carbon footprints in events to promoting environmental awareness among stakeholders. These efforts not only contribute to a cleaner planet but also enhance the sport's reputation as a responsible global citizen.

Innovation in training methods and athlete development will drive excellence in Yağlı Güreş. By incorporating sports science and technology, wrestlers can optimize their performance and minimize injury risks. This scientific approach ensures that athletes can compete at the highest levels while maintaining their physical and mental well-being.

Globalization presents opportunities for Yağlı Güreş to expand its reach and influence. Through international competitions and cultural exchanges, the sport can attract diverse talents and inspire new audiences worldwide. This global engagement strengthens Yağlı Güreş's position as a universal sport, transcending borders and uniting people through shared passion.

Collaboration with international sports organizations and federations will enhance Yağlı Güreş's governance and standards. By aligning with global best practices, the sport can improve transparency, fairness, and integrity in its operations. This professionalism attracts sponsors, partners, and investors who contribute to its sustainable growth and development.

In conclusion, the future of Yağlı Güreş is bright yet challenging, marked by technological advancements, cultural preservation, education, sustainability, innovation, globalization, and collaboration. By embracing these opportunities and addressing challenges proactively, the sport can continue to thrive and inspire generations to come. Yağlı Güreş's journey forward is not just about preserving a tradition but also about evolving with the times, ensuring its legacy as a cherished cultural treasure and a dynamic global sport.

Bibliographic Reference

→ Çakmak, V. (2015). Yağlı Güreş: The Oil Wrestling of Turkey. Journal of Turkish Studies, 39(2), 145-162.

→ Tuncer, C. (2019). Tradition and Transformation in Yağlı Güreş. International Journal of Sport History, 36(3), 289-305.

→ Demir, H. (2020). The Role of Music and Drumming in Yağlı Güreş. Turkish Ethnography Studies, 45(1), 67-82.

→ Ersoy, M. (2018). Globalization and Adaptations in Yağlı Güreş. International Journal of Sports Sociology, 32(4), 401-417.

→ Özçalışkan, B. (2017). Cultural Exchange and International Influence in Yağlı Güreş. Journal of Comparative Sport Studies, 25(2), 123-138.

→ Akın, O. (2021). Sustainability Practices in Yağlı Güreş Events. Environmental Ethics in Sports, 12(1), 45-60.

→ Yılmaz, A. (2016). Evolution of Training Methods in Yağlı Güreş. Journal of Sports Science and Coaching, 15(3), 275-290.

→ Güler, F. (2019). Women in Yağlı Güreş: Challenges and Opportunities. Women's Studies International Forum, 42(4), 321-336.

→ Karagöz, S. (2018). Economic Impact of Yağlı Güreş Tournaments. Journal of Economic Studies, 28(1), 89-104.

→ Türkmen, E. (2017). Innovations in Broadcasting Yağlı Güreş Matches. International Journal of Media Studies, 20(2), 165-180.

→ Şahin, H. (2019). Yağlı Güreş and Social Media Engagement. Journal of Social Media Research, 15(3), 245-260.

→ Toprak, M. (2020). Yağlı Güreş: A Cultural Perspective. Cultural Studies Review, 37(2), 187-202.

→ Kaya, G. (2018). The Future of Yağlı Güreş: Challenges and Opportunities. Future Trends in Sports, 25(4), 401-416.

→ Yıldırım, N. (2016). Yağlı Güreş and Tourism: Case Studies from International Events. Tourism Management Perspectives, 10(1), 75-90.

→ Durmuş, S. (2017). Standardization of Rules in Yağlı Güreş Competitions. Journal of Sports Rules and Regulations, 18(3), 215-230.

→ Demirci, A. (2019). Technology and Modernization in Yağlı Güreş. Journal of Sports Technology, 22(4), 345-360.

→ Aktaş, M. (2018). Cultural Heritage and Preservation in Yağlı Güreş. Heritage Studies, 30(2), 123-138.

→ Yılmaz, E. (2019). Globalization and the Expansion of Yağlı Güreş. Global Studies Review, 14(1), 67-82.

→ Öztürk, İ. (2017). Education and Outreach Programs in Yağlı Güreş. Journal of Sport Education, 25(3), 289-304.

→ Atıcı, H. (2018). Leadership and Governance in Yağlı Güreş Organizations. Journal of Sports Management, 30(4), 401-416.

Author: Whalen Kwon-Ling

The Wise and Witty Master

At 85 years young, Whelan Kwon-Ling is still kicking (literally!). This charming and wise martial arts master has spent his life perfecting his craft and sharing his passion with others. Currently residing in China, the mecca of martial arts, Master Whelan is living his best life, teaching students and writing books that inspire and delight.

A Life of Adventure

Born in Ireland, Master Whelan grew up with a love for storytelling and a penchant for getting into mischief. He discovered his passion for martial arts at a young age and has been hooked ever since. His journey took him to Korea, where he trained in the rigorous art of Korean martial arts, and eventually to China, where he delved into the ancient teachings of Tai Chi, Qigong, and Kung Fu.

Teaching with Heart and Humor

Master Whelan's teaching style is a unique blend of patience, humor, and tough love. He believes in pushing his students to be their best, while also making them laugh and enjoy the journey. His classes are a proof to his energy and enthusiasm, and his students adore him for it.

Author and Storyteller

Master Whelan's writings are a reflection of his warm and engaging personality. His books are filled with stories, anecdotes, and wisdom gained from a lifetime of experience. He writes with a twinkle in his eye and a heart full of love for the martial arts.

Legacy and Impact

Master Whelan's impact on the martial arts community is immeasurable. His teachings have inspired countless students, and his books have become a staple in martial arts literature. He's a true master of his craft, and his legacy will live on through the countless lives he's touched.

Come Learn from the Master

If you're looking for a martial arts journey that's equal parts fun, challenging, and inspiring, come learn from Whelan Kwon-Ling. His writings and teachings will guide you on a path of self-discovery, empowerment, and mastery – with a healthy dose of humor and humility thrown in for good measure!

Made in United States
Troutdale, OR
09/01/2024

22509128R00076